A Quiet Voice

by
Antonia Bissell Laird

DORRANCE & COMPANY
Philadelphia

To Walter J. Laird, Jr. and Alfred E. Bissell
for their love and encouragement

CONTENTS

ACKNOWLEDGMENTS

The author wishes to thank the following for permission to reprint.

"February," "Twelve Past Eight," "Sand," "The Sea," "Night Forest," "Season Song," "Our Highways," "Towers," "Twenty-One," "Middle Age," "Toy Soldiers," "Ninety," and "Anniversary" published in "Time is Moonlight" by the Wilmington Poetry Society and Delaware Writers, Inc. This manuscript was co-winner of the statewide Katherine King Johnson Memorial Poetry Contest for 1967. Copyright Delaware Poetry Center, Sunday, October 22, 1967. Reprinted by permission of the publisher.

"First Snow" published in *The Bulletin* during December 1969; *The Evening And Sunday Bulletin,* Philadelphia. Reprinted by permission of the publisher.

"Wine Tasting" published in *The Bacchus Journal,* Old Lyme, Connecticut. Reprinted by permission of *The Bacchus Journal.*

"Line by Line," "Reopening of the Ford Theatre in Washington," "Death," "Fleeting Dream," "A Forest Walk," "Mist Moon," "Another Wave," "Lies," "Bird Nests," "Lonliness," "Insomnia," "Baloo," "Snow Creatures," and "The Funeral" published in *Delaware Today,* Wilmington, Delaware. Reprinted by permission of the editor.

"Our Highways," and "Season Song" published in *The Garden Club of America Bulletin,* Cleveland, Ohio. Reprinted by permission of *The Garden Club of America Bulletin.*

"End of Summer," "Winter Ice," "Apples," and "Dessert Dream" published in *Gourmet.* Reprinted by permission of the editor.

THE END OF SUMMER

Summer
fades,
and with it goes
sweet white corn,
tomatoes plump with juice,
beans
plucked from the vine,
strawberry mousse,
raspberries
with wine.
Summer's
filled
with watermelon seeds,
blueberries picked
beneath a sharp clear sky,
fresh garden peas,
and rhubarb pie.
Summer's
fled,
pumpkins are sold
from roadside stands.
Fruit is on the trees.
There is a wisp
of frost.
It's time for
basted grouse
and applesauce.

FLEETING DREAM

Desert me not
my fleeting, haunting dream,
for when I wake
reality is just
a breath away.
Linger long
with me
and wrap me well
in lies.
Spin your web
of deep deceit
and promises
a dream can't keep.
For when I wake
this dream won't come
again.
I taste the sweet beginning,
but never grasp
the end.

LINE TO LINE

On your face
life carves
your loves and hates,
with lines depicting
your mistakes
along the way.
Furrows where you frown,
threaded creases
close beside your eyes.

Upon the smooth-skinned map
of youth,
character is slowly brushed.
Truths and lies,
perhaps
the compromise
between the two.

Sleepless nights, unspoken fears,
annoying aches
of later years
add line to line,
but still—
behind the aging face
the young eyes shine.

THE SEA

I know a stretch of lonely beach
where great waves break,
and with their greedy tendrils rake
the pebbles to the sea.

Their shadows etched upon the sand,
the cold rocks rise,
on their crags the seagull cries—
and dives into the sea.

Where crouched behind the clouds the moon
now springs to light,
the darkest heartbeat of the night,
and plunges in the sea.

FIRST SNOW

Beside the house an English Yew,
pillowed down with drifted warmth.
On the Pyracantha hedge,
frozen berries, red to white.

Soft snow weaves a winter cloak,
wraps the garden close inside,
changes colors, sounds and shapes—
Cherry Laurel, dark to light.

High branches of the scarlet oak,
powdered trails against the sky,
while the yellow porch light shines,
snow still falling, day to night.

ASHES

When I die
don't close me in a box,
lowered slowly
into red-brown clay.
You'd have to carry
flowers to my grave
long after spring and I
had fled,
leaving bone
and flesh in dark decay.
I'd rather
give my ashes back to earth,
wrapped in snow
or cradled by a wind.
So when you thought
of me
it wasn't of a stone,
but country walks, white mountains,
and the sea.

ON SEEING *LION IN WINTER*

Queen Eleanor
did hate the king so much
that words spit forth
like venom from her tongue
and falling short, their potency diffused,
hung withered in the air.
What twist of mind
where love and hate combine,
she failing in the one
has lost the other.
Better to have tucked
her heart inside a bracelet
made from swamp-dipped reeds,
and hidden it beside a silvered lake,
while Henry fought his wars and sons
and kissed his paramour awake.

APRIL TREES

Hide me high in the apple tree,
stretch my soul with a strand of bloom.
Petals pale form a bud of pink,
shading fresh from an April loom.

Sing me songs of an endless spring,
wind me warm in the softest breeze.
Swiftly far as the eye can see,
blossoms burst from the April trees.

OLD TREE

Good-bye old tree,
for years I rested
underneath your shade,
where soft moss crept between your roots.
Now they say
that mighty heart has ceased to be.
For generations
rain has licked your leaves,
and snow
has dressed your trunk
with ribs of white.
No more.
Lest lightning throw you
through the attic floor,
strong men are hard at work
with ax and saw.
In this cold world
there is no one to mourn
one passing tree,
except the birds, the squirrels and me.

RAIN

A dark and dreary day.
Rain drips down to form
soft pools on spongy ground.
Window screens are flecked
with rounded drops.
Rain's quick voice resounds
against the roof,
hisses hard at glass.
Damp fingers touch the terrace stone,
caress the grass.
Inside the brown-eared dog and I,
content alone,
my book, his rubber bone.

WAITING FOR SPRING

Waiting
for the shield of clouds
that guards a tender sky,
to catch the whisper of the wind
and ride it by.

Waiting
for the daffodils
to push their slender stalks
above the fresh-turned earth
where sunlight walks.

Waiting
for the softest buds
to settle on the trees—
pussy willows, apple blossoms
bring the golden bees.

FOG

Press close,
enfold me in your damp embrace.
Slide quickly through my tangled hair
and wring it straight.
Force your cheek against
my cringing face,
your cloying breath
upon my neck.
My body shivers
at your touch.
Now grapple at my feet,
I cannot run
for you have bound me well.
There must be fog
like this in Hell.

NIGHT FLIGHT

Lost in an avenue of stars
shining on the compass of the night,
in fragile harmony
we join a shrouded moon
to race the clouds
through a celestial sea.

Cut from the tendrils of the earth,
sailing the far reaches of the sky,
aluminum and steel—
we ride the wings of flight
into the axle
of night's turning wheel.

LONELINESS

Loneliness:
a winding sheet
of sorrow
has bound my heart
today, tonight, tomorrow.
A chill
that wraps around
my arms
and holds me close,
to be depressed, downcast, morose.
An ache
so fierce
it surely would be seen,
but everyone has gone,
the room swept clean.

WINTER ICE

Shimmering in crystal sleeves
spun from threads of brittle ice,
trees beside the country road
bend beneath their frozen load.

High above the wire fence
glistening in a pale cold sun,
frosted apples on a branch
rattle in a wintry dance.

ANOTHER WAVE

Again
another wave
has fled the shore
and curled within itself.
A spray of foam,
sullied by the sand
and rough-shelled company
it keeps.
Cast upon the shore
for one brief wish
in time,
before it's sucked
by sudden fury back
to the soft coddling
of the mother sea.
All blues and greens
and silent deeps.

AN AUGUST DAY

The jet stream pulses through the mackerel clouds,
mares' tails streaming in the cool, clear air.
Sharp winds cut patterns, sweep them high,
blue-white quilting of an August sky.

Barnacles clinging to the cold gray rocks,
sea gulls gliding on a salt-whipped wind.
Canvas filling as the fleet sets sail,
blueberries picked in an old tin pail.

Two boys clamming walk a lonely cove,
footprints fading on the hard-packed sand.
Lobsters boiling to a bright, hot red,
fresh corn roasting in an ember bed.

Cold currents threading through a restless sea,
spray plumes tossing in a high-spun arc.
Waves wearing whitecaps fling them high,
pound the beach beneath an August sky.

WINE TASTING

Around the room
with palates pure.
they sit,
anticipation
waiting on their tongues.
No alcohol
has passed their learned lips,
no nicotine
since noon
has stained their lungs.
With wine-filled glass
they smell the sweet bouquet,
fine Burgundy,
no common Beaujolais.
For nectar's sip
impatiently await
one stalwart friend
who is forever late.
While in the cloakroom
closed in quiet sin,
that errant fellow
bolts ambrosial gin.

NIGHT FOREST

Fir trees etch their shadows in the lake
a lone loon dives;
in the forest stillness cries
the screech owl as it grabs its prey.

Mountains stretch their shoulders to the sky
a sly lynx stalks;
in the velvet darkness walks
the doe beside her speckled fawn.

Thick roots have tangled every path
gray fungus grows;
through the moss on disc-tipped toes
a tree frog steals before the dawn.

SEASON SONG

Icicle dawn has pierced the room
and swept the corners with frosted broom.
Thin and high her silvery wail,
crisp and cold her wintry tale.

Spring has a dancer's whirling feet,
the days grow longer, the blooms fly sweet.
Chilling, then warming breezes blow,
gardeners plant, farmers sow.

Shimmering sun has wrapped the waves
with threads of light in a golden maze.
Hot and low her smoldering song,
deep and sultry summer blows long.

Leaves falling faster fill the sky,
autumn is ending and time sings by.
Sad the honking of geese in flight,
warm the fire and cold the night.

SAND

Sand, sand, sand,
blows everywhere.
Between our toes,
in our clothes,
beneath the petals of a rose.
Sand, sand, sand,
flies through the air,
in our hair—
everywhere
is sand.
It steals
through the house
on the toenails of a mouse
and hides between the sheets.
It creeps.
Vacuums buzz,
brooms sweep,
but sand leaps
into our shoes
and hides.
Summer flies,
and where's the sand?
Hiding in the attic fan,
locked within the suitcase still
until,
sand, sand, sand,
blows everywhere.

THE FUNERAL

Walking straight, a silent row
of mourners
to the funeral go.
People wrapped in memories
and private thoughts.
Prayers they say in church today
have many times
before been said:
the final ceremony
to the dead.
Each one trying not to cry
by thinking of another place
when all their friends alive
and young
saw death wearing an older face.
Clear your throat
it's time to go,
the parting music
has begun.
Soon will be the time to cry
and all alone whisper
good-by.

REOPENING OF THE FORD THEATRE
IN WASHINGTON

They've opened up the theatre,
the house is right across the street.
Quiet, hear the running feet
in April when the seasons meet.

More than a century ago
they carried him across the street,
his heart a faint and failing beat
while buglers blew a sad retreat.

The pillow where they laid his head
is on display across the street.
The coverlet is starched and neat
where once they placed his dusty feet.

I visualize him lying there
in pain across that dry-dirt street,
with candles at his head and feet,
his body stretched out long and neat.

In Washington the flowers bloom
and people walk along that street,
to see the Presidential seat
where Lincoln met his last defeat.

They've opened up the theatre,
the house is right across the street.
Quiet, hear the running feet
in April when the seasons meet.

AUTUMN

Hill after hill has tossed away
pale green leaves of a summer day.
A tapestry has been flung down,
yellow, red, orange veined with brown.

Groves of sunlit evergreen
accent October's fleeting scene.
Splashes of color on the hill
herald the lash of winter's chill.

A FOREST WALK

Still the forest shot with light,
bright sun throws patterns on the ground,
on lacy fern and moulding log
shafts of gold run up and down.

Coolness filters through the trees,
a green snake glides without a sound,
above a shaded stagnant pool
dragonflies spin round and round.

COME DANCE WITH ME

Waltz with me,
I feel the music
running through my feet,
a captivating beat
that leads me on.
Whirl with me
across a polished floor,
your arm around my waist,
your steps in tune.
Soar with me,
I hear the violins
around my head.
Chandeliers spin by.
Music and its lilting beat.
Come dance with me,
you men
with magic feet.

DEATH

Death curls waiting in an easy chair,
softly purring
in a warm cat way.
Relaxed and yawning
till the day dawns fair,
slowly stretching,
grasps you unaware.

Death runs quickly on a padded paw,
harshly breathing
in the sick-filled room.
Watchful, demanding
what is his full share,
sternly choosing
in the cool night air.

Death comes lightly on a wing-shaped leaf,
swiftly lifted
on a crisp fall day.
Quietly taking
into his cold care
the young, the old,
the ugly, the fair.

BALOO

A German Shepherd

Grow old along with me my gray-tipped friend,
your muzzle whitened by the breath of age.
Stretch close beside me while the fire burns
and let me scratch behind your silk-soft ear.

Your proud head resting on two tired paws,
a ruff of grizzled fur around your neck.
In dreams you chase the echo of your youth
when other dogs before you passed in fear.

Kipling's Baloo ruled his jungle world,
but you are master of a human heart.
So lie beside me while the day grows dim
and let me scratch behind your silk-soft ear.

LIES

Lies
can trap you deeper
as they curl around your tongue.
Guile and clever cunning
in a web
that words have sung.
Ensnare you in an abyss,
in a tangled net of holes,
binding you astutely
in deceiving pleats and folds.
Lies
can suffocate you
before the trap is sprung,
making you a person
that you wished you'd not become.
Hiding in the shadows
behind the face of truth,
neglecting neither wrinkled age
nor sanguine youth.

DRY LEAVES

Rustling through
the dry leaves of my mind
are bits of verse,
the rest are lost in time.
A song
without the opening line,
a face without a name,
a book
whose ending I cannot forget.
Children playing
in the sun.
Poetry I'll write
but haven't yet begun.
Laughter
with your hand in mine.
Sad days
with somber thoughts,
days when life rings fair.
But you my love
through all the leaves
are everywhere.

FEBRUARY

Magic moon,
your gleaming rays have loosed the golden stars
and touched the corners of a midnight sky
with silver threads.
You scatter moonbeams, hurling them to earth,
and change the shadows into silken nets
for winter's breath
to fill with flakes of February snow.

TWELVE PAST EIGHT

They're late,
the operation was for eight—
it's now twelve past.
The stretcher's cold.
They've strapped me down
and gone
to hide behind a gown
of green or blue.
On the wall the clock
before my eyes
ticks on.

I've passed this way before
and yet
it all seems strange.
The fear, the icy sweat,
the wait.
The thought that sometime
all must die
but not today.

The brilliant lights,
the eyes that smile
behind the mask.
How far away
the quiet voice that says
to count to ten,
and then
the pounding in my head is gone
and on the wall
the clock ticks on.

OUR HIGHWAYS

Darkness, the coverlet of night
embroidered with stars,
cloaking in silvered shadows
the highways and their cars;

dimming the billboards' message
along the twist of road
where bottles, cans and Kleenex
in carelessness are sowed;

veiling the sun's bright harshness
with twilight's purple skies
until man's ugly junkyards
are wrapped in dusk's disguise.

TOWERS

Giants wearing welded steel
cross the meadows one by one,
crushing down the buttercups—
monsters walking in the sun;

voltage shooting through their arms,
massive strength in every vein,
on a power-driven march
down a ruined country lane.

FOURTEEN

Fourteen
is frustrating,
no adolescent game.
Gone the idle childhood,
parents aren't the same.
Angry and impatient,
wanting to be old.
Inside feeling anxious,
outside acting bold.

Fourteen
is a turning,
away from what has passed.
The future lies before you
waiting to be cast.
Inside feeling older,
outside looking young.
Quick to be the chorus
for songs that others sung.

TWENTY-ONE

What fun life's been,
each day I greet the world
as though it just
were made for me
and no one else.
I'm free
to work, to play, and if I choose
to take a boat, a plane
and fly away
today.
There's so much I must see,
to ski
beneath the Matterhorn,
or take a camera
into Kenya,
shoot a rhinoceros at play.
Rome calls to me
with all its Latin tongue
to come
and visit old Pompeii
and sail the Grecian isles
as Homer did
when he was young.
How full life's been,
each party has been fun.
Why do I feel that youth flies by
because I'm twenty-one?

MIDDLE AGE

Time is running through our hourglass
as sand blows now across the dunes,
and oceans' waters lick the shores
to play their endless, ageless tunes.

Time is moonlight through our fingers,
never captured though we run
to hold it as it shimmers by
from sun to moon, from moon to sun.

Time is happiness or sorrow
captured in life's golden cage,
every moment, pain or pleasure,
dances past in middle age.

NINETY

Please stay and talk,
you see
the nights are long
and sleep's forgotten me.

I've come full circle,
now a child again,
a nurse to pull the blinds
and close the door.

Visitors are few
because
my friends have died:
I've been to funerals one by one.

I've lived
too long but death won't come.
I ramble on,
I know,

the words sound strange
as though a foreign tongue
had placed them in my mouth.

There's someone whispering by my ear,
a gentle voice,
but pain and fear
confront me arm in arm.
Alone I fight them through the night
till dawn.

ANNIVERSARY

Through trees we planted long ago
moonlight has found your treasured face,
erased the lines of sixty years
and wrapped our love in moon-leaf lace.

Your eyes a mirthful brilliant blue
still laugh with me though youth has fled,
and for a moment years slip back:
you're the young man that I wed.

Now the jealous pouting clouds
have chased the moonlight from my eye,
you hum an old forgotten tune
but so do I.

INSOMNIA

Every breath you take
accentuates
your envelope of sleep,
while I lie here
with nerve ends stretched
to capture weightlessness.
My mind a nest of insects
so engrossed
with senseless thoughts.
All small sounds caught
and magnified,
an angry fly,
the shower's drip,
the loud vibrating hum
of the electric clock.
I reach the light
in angry sleeplessness
to read the final chapter
of my book,
and then
I feel a numbing yawn.
Perhaps I'll sleep
before the first
bleak streak of dawn.

SNOW CREATURES

A prehistoric Brontosaurus,
thrusting neck
and bulbous nose,
was waiting by the forest path
to grab a snowshoe
rabbit
racing past.
Next to him a giant elf
on a shaggy creature's back
was laughing
to himself.
A monstrous bear
reared high
upon strong bulging legs
and raised his paw.
Fir trees dressed in masquerade.
I saw
footprints
all around.
Who has
dared
to walk across
this snow-rilled ground?

LOST LOVE

Lost love,
I saw you in the looking glass
behind my head,
reached quickly for your hand
to find instead
an empty room.
I walked the city street—
a profile in a shop was you,
full face
the eyes were brown not blue.
An arm brushed mine
to catch me unaware,
the smile was kind—
yours spun laughter out of air.
At night I hold you close,
reality is far away.
All too soon
the dawn, the day.

DESSERT DREAM

Serve me Charlotte Malakoff,
stiff with well-stirred almond cream.
Apples in a warm cake roll,
hard sauce in a silver bowl.

Lemon pudding browned on top,
lady fingers shaped with care.
Soufflé laced with Grand Marnier,
crème caramel renversée.

Apricots well soaked and strained,
blended in a frothy whip.
Orange jelly in a mold,
tarte aux fraises, soft custard cold.

Thin crêpes filled with sweet preserves,
peaches brandied, pears well poached.
Grapes nestling in sour cream,
meringues in a spun sugar dream.

Forget soup, entrée and fish,
vegetables prepared with herbs.
Puff pastries go floating by,
Napoleons have caught my eye.

TOY SOLDIERS

Through cobwebbed windows drifting dust,
dawn comes courting soft and shy
and sweeps the shadows from the sill
where all the broken soldiers lie.

Where once the troops of England marched,
a blazing regiment in red,
with fife and bravely beating drum
the only color now is lead.

The brave young men in Federal blue,
the gallant band in tattered gray
who fought for honor, love and land
have fallen now in disarray.

And those that fought the Kaiser's hun
and Hitler's strong and booted troop
before the ravaging of time
have fallen in a khaki group.

Through cobwebbed windows drifting dust,
dusk comes creeping soft and shy
and spreads the shadows on the sill
where all the broken soldiers lie.

MOUNTAIN WILDFLOWERS

Yellow paints the Buttercups,
streaks the purple Columbine,
pencils color
on a Cutleaf Daisy's face.
Shines on sturdy Dandelions,
Primrose, Long-Stalked Balsamroot,
wraps the common Goldenrod
in feathered lace.
Blue Alpine Forget-Me-Not,
Lupine nodding in a field,
lavender the Clematis
with slender vine.
Sticky Pink Geranium,
Creeping Berried Wintergreen,
Dusty Maidens
blushing in a soft pink line.
Wild Hyacinths, Spring Beauties
by an overhanging ledge,
Mountain Bluebells
blooming near the water's edge.
Delphinium and Larkspur,
Early Paintbrush dipped in red,
uncultivated beauty
in a Rocky Mountain bed.

THE TETONS

Sharp against
a blue Wyoming sky,
the Teton mountains rise
in rock-hewn splendor
from the wooded valley floor.
Cathedral peaks
thrust high
their steep arêtes,
white ridged with snow
in mid-July.
Jagged
as a giant's tooth
they bite the clouds.
Through rains and winds
for countless centuries
they'll stand;
princely guards
above a vast uncluttered land.

BIRDS' NESTS

Now
with trees stripped bare,
the birds' nests everywhere
are starkly hung
against
a cold November sky.
Their summer spent unseen,
well-hidden by a windowshade
of sun-splashed green,
to be exposed
as autumn flees.
Precariously perched
above
a gray and rain-washed world,
they wait for spring
to bring
the birds.

LOVE

Love
delicate as a slender
thread of dew
upon the grass.
Lace of cobwebs
shattered by a broom.
Milkweed pods
that fly before the wind,
rose petals
falling in a heated room.

Love
strong as the skein
that binds my life
to yours.
Your steady heartbeat
underneath my head.
My arms to take
your love
and hold it close,
through tides of dreams
till we as one awake.

SPANISH MOSS

Hide the witches' shiny pates,
their wigs hang listless in the trees,
they must haunt the bayou groves
and wrap their heads in Smilax leaves.

Black mud oozing through their toes
they laugh a high and crackling sound,
where moccasins in anger crawl
and ring the ground for miles around.

Long ago a witches' dance,
how black the night, how carved the moon,
wild gyrations, whispered spells,
gray crones torturing a loon.

Beneath the forest deathly still
incarnation, evil rite,
poisonberries stirred with sticks
all practiced on one wicked night.

When the morning came at last
the oaks had stolen clear away—
the witches trailing hanks of hair,
the moss that covers them today.

Hide the witches' shiny pates
their wigs hang listless in the trees,
they must haunt the bayou groves
and wrap their heads in Smilax leaves.

EVERYONE

Everyone is telling
me their troubled thoughts.
I do not want to hear
but they talk on
until I can not tell
one story from another
in my ear.
Everyone is whispering
scandal to me now.
I recognize the voices
and the name.
How strange it seems,
I've heard it all before
it sounds the same.
I do not want to play
their idle game.
Everyone is thinking
things for me to do.
I wish they'd cease
their chattering and talk.
I'd rather walk
alone across a field.
Everyone is nibbling
parts of me away,
until there will be nothing
left for anyone.
I plead leave me alone
but no one hears.
And so the nights turn into days
and months to years.

TOO LATE

On Tudor windows' shrouded panes
the dirt of twenty years remains.
No laughing children come to play
among the weeds of dank decay.

The balustrade has fallen down,
the whining wind the only sound
through rooms where family portraits hung,
where wine was served and carols sung.

Gray field mice scurry to and fro
where we as children used to go.
Thin cobwebs garlanding the hall,
Flock paper shredding off the wall.

Old floorboards rot beneath my shoe
the fireplace lays darkened too.
The brass andirons used to shine
when you were twelve and I was nine.

Behind me now I close the gate,
I've stayed too long, I've come too late.
But childhood memories came to play
among the dust of dark decay.

THE LABRADOR

Across the rows of drying corn,
through marshy field and tangled vine
the hunter in a blue-black coat,
with eyes reflecting yellow light
has picked the middle of the night
to chase the moon.

From his cedar-smelling bed,
with panting tongue he's watched the ball
that bounces on the evening clouds.
Now he sees it straight ahead,
tucked beside the river bed,
he splashes in.

The Labrador with mud-dipped paws
shakes the river from his ears
and licks the moon drops off his nose.
The hunter has no keen regret,
he's chased the moon and found him wet,
he'll try again!

PATTERNS

Look down
from flying high,
see knitted squares of land
unraveling
beneath an empty sky.
Patterns
everywhere,
in rows of trees
around a farm,
plowed fields
and those stripped bare,
gold wheat and corn.
Round ponds
and rippled lakes,
mountains
tipped in snow.
Wild parklands
spreading free,
swamp lands and rivers
snaking toward a distant sea.
Patterns
everywhere,
in shade and sun,
in shapes and squares
of land.
Rough rocks, soft earth
and sand
that shimmers
underneath an empty sky.

THE CHIPMUNK

What misdirected nerve
in your small brain
has sent this foolish message
to your feet?
Brown Chipmunk
in a cold-lashed land
of snow.
While you slept
all curled in body warmth,
the world turned white
and left your summer meadows
deep below.
Small one,
go back to sleep.
Cruel winds dart
crystal needles
at your cheeks.
No friend
but hungry foes await.
Bigger paw prints
mark the woods than yours.
Quick now, beneath
the snow,
until the warm winds bring
the dampish smells
of early spring.

POSSUM

Possum by the roadside
lying still,
last night when you
had gone to hunt,
your name was struck
from Nature's multiplying list.
Now paws outstretched
as though asleep,
you've not been missed.
Let others finish up
the hunt tonight.
Run, scuttle, leap
across the road,
pursued by grinding monsters
belching fumes,
strong blinking eyes that light
the asphalt way.

FIFTY YEARS

What will we find
to talk about when fifty years have passed,
or will my mind
have faded into yours?
The sweet old couple
in the paper holding hands
half a century ago were wed;
if one should die
the other might as well be dead.
They know each other's foibles,
every virtue that they lack,
yet have no inclination
to fight the other back.
Thoughts are interwoven,
strong opinions turned to gray,
wrapped up in the memory of
one long yesterday.

THE CIRCLE

Life turns slowly
birth to death,
youth to age
is swiftly swept.
Where the toddler used to hide,
man is measuring his stride.
What you were is what I am,
the man the child, the child the man.
Find me now a quiet place
where old is old without disgrace.
Birth to death
and youth to age,
unwinding on a turning page.

ADIRONDACK MOMENT

Bunchberries crouch at the base of the trees,
gray lichen clings to the sides.
High in a tall fir, cheeks bulging fat,
a small chipmunk angrily chides.

A flutter of birch leaves close to the lake
whisper their song through the wood.
Hemlock and balsam boughs sweep to the ground,
perfuming the air where they've stood.

Green moss grows rampant in soft spongy mounds,
toadstools wear cushiony hats.
Just as the moonlight first touches the shores
it brushes the wings of two bats.

WORDS

Over and under,
above and beyond,
words are like geese
as they wing from the pond.
Exquisitely lovely, incredibly soft,
carrying the mystery
of language aloft.
Words filled with gravel,
those coated to soothe,
wretchedly harsh,
esthetically smooth.
Phlegmatically stolid,
shamelessly bold,
lavishly rich,
piercingly cold.
Whimsical, literal, sensitive sound,
words are the history
to which we are bound.

A.E.B.

A true Elizabethan man,
love of power, love of land.
A mind to house in brilliant thought
the stocks he's sold, the stocks he's bought.

Words fall quickly as he talks,
ruddy cheeks, a rapid walk.
Out Stockford Road at five A.M.
to Market Street by seven ten.

A temper held by steel control,
a tender heart, a sportsman's soul.
A bugler with his horn held high,
to trout, a wiley, clever guy.

Dickens, Conrad, Kipling's "Kim"
is where his love of books begin.
Durant, Christie, Gibbon's "Fall,"
the old, the new, he's read them all.

Silver tankards, Gaudy Dutch,
his pleasures never cost him much!
Norway's salmon, Scotland's moors,
are not without their Bissell lures.

Dynamic, charming, thoughtful too,
with eyes a pale but piercing blue.
To A.E.B. at sixty-five
a toast, there's no man more alive.

MIST MOON

Drift moon
mysteriously veiled
in mist that swirls
around the shadows
on a city street.

Drift moon
riding the evening sky
through murky clouds
that chase cool autumn
rains as they retreat.

Drift moon
above the darkening night,
pale hands of light
to bind the echo
of my running feet.

APPLES

Apples
in a green-edged bowl
hold the warmth of morning sun,
waiting for the paring knife
to slice them thin
for pie.
Apples
quartered to be stuffed
in a wild and well-hung duck.
Apples cut in one-inch
rings to fry.
Apple Dumplings, Apple Crisp,
butter, cinnamon and cloves.
Apple crescents on a plate
with Stilton cheese.
Apples
by the bushel load
taste of sap and summer sun,
harvested beneath
an autumn sky.